This book belongs to

_____

...the apple of God's eye!

EMBRACING THE LOVE
OF THE FATHER

"I am the apple of His eye
He is the core of my being"

Vera LeRay Warner

Includes Study Companion and Journal

IN HIS IMAGE
PUBLISHING
Cocoa, FL

P.O. Box 236552 Cocoa, FL 32923

Warner, Vera LeRay

Embracing the Love of the Father

ISBN: 978-0-9713072-7-8

DEDICATION

I dedicate this book to Diana Nicoson, a long time friend, partner in ministry and one of my many "spiritual daughters."

May you embrace the love of the Father like never before.

CONTENTS

ACKNOWLEDGMENTS

I wish to thank Chaplain Steve and Brenda Sexton for extending the gracious invitation to minister to the women of the Hessen area Protestant Women of the Chapel. You guys started this whole thing!

I offer thanks to the anointed prayer warriors-the commanders of the First Watch; Lorraine, Holly, Roderick, Erica, Carmen, Yvonne, Lillie, Birgit, Patricia, Angela, Greg and Dana. Your prayer covering is a blessing to me.

Thank you to Dr. Marilyn Chipman. Your editing skills and suggestions are like gold to me. Your encouragement is such a blessing.

Finally, to the finest man who ever walked the planet, my husband, Michael. Honey, I love you and thank you so much for your unrelenting support. You are the best!

FOREWORD

One of the great joys of ministering to others is to watch them mature into *"Great Warriors"*. Vera is such a warrior. Having had the privilege of being her Pastor in Hawaii, I count it a great joy to recommend her work to you. Soon you will discover, as I have, that Vera has a passion for the things of our Lord.

There are several things that one will notice upon the study of Vera Warner's latest work, *"Embracing the Love of the Father"*. This writer takes us on a journey of sorts through the *"Orchard of history"*. We are invited, even enticed to meticulously walk through this orchard and pick fruit from the rich resources of God's Word. Any true student of the Word will discover quickly that with care this writer leads us into a crucial study using Israel as the *"Centerpiece"*. As the writer states too many of God's people are in *"emotional lockdown"* and do not even know it.

With care and compassion the writer reveals the love and grace of a loving father toward His creation. Systematically the writer reveals that God's plan is one of *producing, providing and protecting* that which belongs to Him. In the following pages, one will discover that they are on a journey of recognition. This walk through the Word of God reveals a *purpose and a plan* for their life. As we walk through this orchard of understanding, we discover that there is a watchful eye over us. We turn our gaze upward and we discover that it is the *"loving creator"*. As we look closer we see something in His eyes. *To our amazement, it is us. We are the apple of His eye.*

Take the nourishment that comes from this work. Eat every word. Herein you will discover that you are *"precious fruit"* to the Heavenly Father. Rest in the fact that God loves you beyond what your mind can comprehend. Enjoy!

Pastor Roger Powell
Word of Grace Tabernacle
McDonough, Georgia

PREFACE

I had been invited to be the speaker at the Hessen Area Protestant Women of the Chapel Spring Retreat. During the course of preparing my messages I felt that, as part of my outline, I was to use the Scripture reference in Psalm 17:8 – *"Keep me as the apple of your eye; hide me under the shadow of your wings"*. As I began to ponder this verse I heard the Father speak to me ever so gently, "You are one of my apple girls." It was one of those light bulb moments. You know those moments when the Lord just suddenly drops an idea in your spirit. What a sweet, funny and comforting concept. So I did a little research and found that there are at least 2500 different varieties of apples in the United States and 7500 varieties world wide. The varieties are different in flavor and texture and color and yet they are all apples. From the red delicious to the fuji, to the honey crunch and the firm, tart granny smith, the apple is loaded with nutritional value and is one of the most favored fruit of all time. Thank God for the apple!

"You are one of my apple girls" was the springboard for the whole idea of "God's Apple Lady – G.A.L". We are the apple of the Father's eye. We are God's ladies. We are His well mannered and considerate women with high standards of proper behavior. And yet we are also His gals, those informal creatures that are lovely and funny and spontaneous and a joy to be with and to be around.

Next came the idea of this book. So many of God's Apple Ladies love Him but cannot fully accept His love for them. So many of His precious gals are not completely assured of who they are or where they stand with the Father so it makes it difficult for them to fully embrace His love.

Well, G.A.L.s, it is my prayer that by the time you finish this book that you would have come to the place where you may deny yourself many things in this life, but not the love of the Father. By the time you finish this book may you truly be able to confess with confidence, "I am the apple of His eye: but He is the core of my being!"

Vera LeRay Warner
Zotzenbach, Germany
August, 2007

HOW TO USE THE STUDY COMPANION AND JOURNAL

The *Embracing the Love of the Father* study companion and journal has been incorporated in this book. This study companion has been designed to assist the reader in discovering the love of God, afresh and anew, and accepting His love without reservation and giving His love without hesitation.

It can be used either in a small study group setting or by an individual during personal devotion and study time. It can readily be adapted to both.

Each chapter is formatted in much the same way as it will contain the following six sections:

- Central Idea of the Chapter
- Commentary on the Chapter
- Questions for Reflection
- Application
- Closing Statement
- Prayer

There is also a journaling section where you can write down those things that the Father specifically whispers to your heart; those personal things that will become valuable nuggets that you can refer to time and again in the coming days ahead.

If you are a leader in a small group setting it is suggested that you do more intensive study to be able to supply more information than is given during the commentary on each chapter. You would then go through the questions with the group allowing them to give their answers.

Before you begin:

- Pray that God would give you revelation and show you ways to apply what you will learn in a very practical manner.
- Read the passages of scripture suggested more than once to get a clearer understanding of what is being conveyed.

During the course of your study:

- Write down your answers as it will aid in memory retention.
- Don't forget to write your reflective thoughts in the journaling section. God will speak to you and it will be a joy writing down what He says when He speaks.

INTRODUCTION

In the years that I have walked with my Lord, from time to time I have come in contact with women of God who loved the Lord and who were doing their best to live holy lives before Him and yet the peace and joy that only He can give seemed to elude them. These precious women of God would sit in church Sunday after Sunday, attend prayer meetings and Bible studies and Sunday school, and work whenever and wherever they were needed. Yet they always seemed to be only "almost there." They never seemed able to enter into more than marginal intimacy with the Father. Their love relationship with the Father seemed sporadic at best.

For years I couldn't understand why some would go to deliverance session after deliverance session and yet the problem was still evident. I was given the privilege to form relationship with a few of these precious women and, in getting to know them, I discovered that there seemed to be a common thread that ran in the course of each of their lives; they either could not or would not allow themselves to be completely enraptured by the love of the Father. There seemed to be an emotional lockdown. For whatever reason there were walls that had been built in their emotions, perhaps due to the relationships experienced or a lack of relationships with their earthly fathers or other men in their lives. Oh, they knew of the love of God and they truly loved the Lord, but at the same time they seemed stuck and could never allow themselves to go beyond recognition of the love of the Father. They could never allow themselves to be completely enraptured by love that is so powerful and so awesome and so freely given. The Scripture says, *"There is no fear in love; but perfect love casts out fear, because fear involves torment. But he who fears has not been made perfect in love." 1 John 4: 18*

Are you one of God's precious women who are stuck? Does someone you know seem to be stuck in that place called, "afraid to be loved by the Father"? If you are, then my prayer is that as you read each page God will minister in such a way that you will allow him free access to every area of your heart. He can bring to surface and heal those things in your emotions that have prevented you from allowing Him to love you. If you know of others who are in this place, may you gain better understanding of how to pray for them that they would be healed, so that the love of the Father would permeate every fiber of their being and that they would truly abide in His peace and joy.

THERE WAS A WORM IN MY APPLE

Here I am in the orchard of life
Waiting and yearning for a day without strife.
There's a worm in my apple.

How'd he get there; I haven't a clue
Oh me, oh my what do I do
I am so tired of going through,
There's a worm in my apple.

God made all creatures both great and small.
But, I don't care for this one at all.
It will be the cause of my great fall.
There's a worm in my apple.

He's eating away at that which is mine.
Oh, Father help me please give me a sign,
some relief I long to find.
There's a worm in my apple.

He's an intruder, a parasite, he doesn't belong.
He's eating away and stealing my song.
Oh, for deliverance; I long and I long.
There's a worm in my apple.

From the outside I still look rather okay,
I so desperately wanting to keep it at bay.
Lord, help me now is what I pray.
I don't want this worm in my apple.

One word from you, Lord and I will be free.
Set free to be made what you want me to be.
I don't want to be blind, I want to see!
I had a worm in my apple.

Oh, look at me now all shiny and new.
To that worm I say, "I am done with you."
I know it was My Father who brought me through.
No more worm in my apple!

Embracing the Love of the Father: From Recognition to Understanding

For this reason I bow my knees to the Father of our Lord Jesus Christ, from whom the whole family in heaven and earth is named, that He would grant you, according to the riches of His glory, to be strengthened with might through His Spirit in the inner man, that Christ may dwell in your hearts through faith; that you, being rooted and grounded in love, may be able to comprehend with all the saints what is the width and length and depth and height— to know the love of Christ which passes knowledge; that you may be filled with all the fullness of God.
Ephesians 3: 14-19 (NKJV)

I cannot even remember exactly when I was first made aware of the fact that God exists and that He loves me. Perhaps it was as I sat as a child in the back yard of Mrs. Turner and she served us kids cookies and kool-aid and told us story after story from the Bible. Or perhaps it was as I sat in that small Sunday school classroom and they showed us a film of the crucifixion of Christ. The truth is that it feels like I have always known that God exists and that He loves me. You know children have the ability to just accept by faith those things with which the adult mind struggles. As with the majority of us, the problem seldom has been whether or not we are loved by God, but going beyond that fact and accepting and embracing His love. God's desire is so much more than a mere recognition of His love. His desire is that we go from awareness to understanding.

The word "recognition" is defined as "awareness or an acknowledgment". We witness account after account of how God revealed himself to the nation of Israel and through His revelation to them they became keenly aware and recognized His love for them. God, in turn, has revealed His love for us through His Son and the work of Calvary and we, too, become keenly aware of and recognize His love. We initially accept His love by entering into a love

relationship with Him, but for so many the relationship does not continue to grow as it should and many find themselves "stuck" in a place of not abiding in that love. It is almost like going around and around on the merry-go-round of life; reaching for the brass ring and not ever being able to grasp it. God desires that we go further than recognition of His love to an understanding of His love. To understand means to know thoroughly by close contact. It also means to grasp or to comprehend. Comprehension has to do with the senses or our feelings. The Father wants us to feel the love that He has for us. He desires to touch our emotions with His love and enrapture us so much so that it will cause us to accept Him fully and to embrace Him fully. God is love.

In Ephesians the third chapter the Apostle Paul writes to the saints in Ephesus that the mystery of Christ which had been long hidden was revealed to him. That mystery was that we (the Gentiles) would become fellow-heirs in Christ. Jews and Gentiles would now be the body of Christ equally serving together. He went on further to pray that they would have greater comprehension of the love of the Father. Let's examine more closely what the apostle said…

"For this reason I bow my knees to the Father of our Lord Jesus Christ, from whom the whole family in heaven and earth is named, that He would grant you according to the riches of His glory to be

strengthened with might through His Spirit in the **inner man**,

The Greek word for **strengthened** is krataio/omai and it means to be strong, but not just to be strong but to increase in intensity. It means to grow.

The Greek word for **inner man** is eásw and it means the internal soul or the conscience, which is that part of us that, through an awareness of something, has an affect on our conduct. The conscience governs our thoughts and our actions.

that Christ may **dwell** in your hearts through faith

The Greek word for **dwell** is katoikeÑw and it means inhabitor. Christ literally comes in and inhabits. It means to live in, reside in, to fill.

> that you being **rooted and grounded** in love, may be able to **comprehend** with all the saints what is the width and length and depth and height—

To be **rooted and grounded** means to be established and to be established means to be recognized and accepted and placed in a secure position.

The Greek word for **comprehend** is katalamba/nw and it means to lay hold of with the mind; to understand, perceive, learn and comprehend.

> to **know** the love of Christ which passes knowledge;

The Greek word for **know** is ginwñskw and it means to learn to know, come to know, get a knowledge of, perceive, feel to know, understand, have knowledge of, to understand

> that you may be **filled** with all the **fullness** of God.

The Greek word for **filled** is plhro/w and it means to make full, to fill up, i.e. to fill to the full; to cause to abound, to furnish or supply liberally (I abound, I am liberally supplied).

The Greek word for **fullness** is plh/rwma and it means fullness, abounding, abundance, and completeness.

Now, let's read Ephesians 3: 16-19 from the Amplified Version.

> *May He grant you out of the rich treasury of His glory to be strengthened and reinforced with mighty power in the inner man by the [Holy] Spirit [Himself indwelling your innermost being and personality]. May Christ through your faith [actually] dwell (settle down, abide, make His permanent home) in your hearts! May you be rooted deep in love and founded securely on love, That you may have the power and be strong to apprehend*

and grasp with all the saints [God's devoted people, the experience of that love] what is the breadth and length and height and depth [of it]; [That you may really come] to know [practically, through experience for yourselves] the love of Christ, which far surpasses mere knowledge [without experience]; that you may be filled [through all your being]unto all the fullness of God [may have the richest measure of the divine Presence, and become a body wholly filled and flooded with God Himself]!
Ephesians 3: 16-19 Amplified Bible

Yes, it is emphatically God's intention that we go from recognition and acknowledgment of His love to greater understanding and full acceptance of His love. Our God, who is love, wants to lavish His Holy love upon us and in us and through us in such a way that we are totally and completely smitten. He wants us to be so affected by His love that we are awestruck in His presence.

Chapter One

From Recognition to Understanding

Central Theme
God's will for us is that we not only recognize that He loves us, but that we also cultivate a deep understanding of His love and accept His love and embrace it.

The Word of God says, "Except you are converted and become as little children…"Matthew 18:3 NKJV Children have the ability just to accept by faith those things with which the adult mind struggles. Children just seem to be little sponges when it comes to accepting and embracing the love given them. As adults so many struggle not so much with the fact that God really does love them, but their struggle is usually with accepting and embracing His love. We recognize or are aware of His love for us and we even acknowledge it, but the Father wants more for His daughters. His desire for us is much more than mere recognition. His desire for you is to go from awareness to understanding.

1. Write down, in your own words, a definition of what it means to recognize something.

_____

_____

_____

_____

2. Write down, in your own words, a definition of what it means to understand.

_____

_____

_____

_____

3. What is the difference between the two?

_____

_____

_____

_____

_____

4. When do you remember becoming keenly aware of the love of God?

_____

_____

_____

_____

_____

_____

5. Turn in your Bible to Ephesians the third chapter and read the entire chapter at least five times.

6. In verses 14 -19 there are at least four things that the Apostle Paul prayed that God would grant you. Write down those four things.

_____

_____

_____

_____

_____

7. Now explain, to the best of your ability, these four things.

_____

_____

_____

_____

_____

_____

_____

_____

_____

_____

_____

_____

_____

_____

_____

APPLICATION...

8. Write an honest self-assessment of your recognition of the love of the Father.

_____

_____

_____

_____

_____

9. Write an honest self-assessment of your understanding of the love of your heavenly Father.

_____

_____

_____

_____

_____

10. What type of man is (or was if he is no longer living) your earthly Father? Explain the relationship that you have or had with him.

_____

_____

_____

_____

_____

_____

11. Do you feel that your view of your earthly Father has had an impact on your understanding and acceptance of the love of your heavenly Father? If so explain.

_____

_____

_____

_____

_____

_____

_____

_____

_____

_____

_____

Yes, it is emphatically God's intention that we go from recognition and acknowledgment of His love to greater understanding and full acceptance of His love. Our God, who is love, wants to lavish His Holy love upon us and in us and through us in such a way that we are totally and completely smitten. He wants us to be so affected by His love that we are awestruck in His presence.

Prayer

Father, please forgive me for being afraid to allow you to love me as you want to. Father I ask you to heal me of all wounds that would cause me to have a distorted view of your love for me. Please correct my spiritual vision and increase my understanding of your love and cause me to accept your love for me and embrace it with all my heart. In Jesus Name, Amen.

JOURNALING

(Now write down those things that come to your mind as you reflect upon this lesson. It may help to go back over the questions and the responses.)

_____

_____

_____

_____

_____

_____

_____

_____

_____

_____

_____

_____

_____

_____

_____

_____

_____

_____

_____

_____

_____

_____

_____

Embracing the Love of the Father: Looking to Israel, Our Example

Moreover, brethren, I do not want you to be unaware that all our fathers were under the cloud, all passed through the sea, all were baptized into Moses in the cloud and in the sea, all ate the same spiritual food, and all drank the same spiritual drink. For they drank of that spiritual Rock that followed them, and that Rock was Christ. But with most of them God was not well pleased, for their bodies were scattered in the wilderness. Now these things became our examples, to the intent that we should not lust after evil things as they also lusted.
1 Corinthians 10: 1-6

One of the ways that we can come to a place of greater understanding of God's infinite love is to look back and study or examine the love relationship that He had with the children of Israel. I believe that it is safe to say that God intended for us, the "New Testament" Church, to look to the "Church in the Wilderness" as an example or a pattern (in some aspects) for the church of today.

In 2 Timothy 3:15-16 Paul says that, *"...and that from childhood you have known the Holy Scriptures, which are able to make you wise for salvation through faith which is in Christ Jesus. All Scripture is given by inspiration of God and is profitable for doctrine; for reproof, for correction, for instruction in righteousness"*. Paul could not have been referring exclusively to New Testament Scripture because, at the time of writing this letter to Timothy, the New Testament was in the process of being written and/or examined for authenticity and authoritative content. Paul had to be speaking about the Old Testament law. It was the Old Testament Law that Timothy had studied as a child. Also in 1 Corinthians the 10th chapter, Paul specifically states that the history of the nation of Israel serves as an example for the church. Having said this, let's examine what is revealed to us about the love relationship that God intended and that He had with the children of Israel and what it means for the New Testament Church today.

For you are a people holy to the LORD your God. The LORD your God has chosen you out of all the peoples on the face of the earth to be his people, his treasured possession. The LORD did not set his affection on you and choose you because you were more numerous than other peoples, for you were the fewest of all peoples. But it was because the LORD loved you and kept the oath he swore to your forefathers that he brought you out with a mighty hand and redeemed you from the land of slavery, from the power of Pharaoh king of Egypt. Know therefore that the LORD your God is God; he is the faithful God, keeping his covenant of love to a thousand generations of those who love him and keep his commands.
Deuteronomy 7: 6-9 (NIV)

God's original intention for the children of Israel was first and foremost that they enter into a "Covenant of Love" with him. God chose them for no other reason except that He loved them. I think about sports and how we choose the ones to be on our team who are the strongest or the fastest. If it comes to academics, the ones who are chosen are usually the smartest or the brightest.

But Israel was not chosen for any of the aforementioned, but simply because God set His love upon them, and He had made a promise. That is why He singled them out and placed His hand upon them, and for no other reason. It is almost as if God purposely chose the underdog so that He could use their insufficiency to prove to them that He was God.

Remember the days of old; consider the generations long past. Ask your father and he will tell you, your elders, and they will explain to you. When the Most High gave the nations their inheritance, when he divided all mankind, he set up boundaries for the peoples according to the number of the sons of Israel. For the LORD's portion is his people, Jacob his allotted inheritance. In a desert land he found him, in a barren and howling waste. He shielded him and cared for him; he guarded him as the apple of his eye, like an eagle that stirs up its nest and hovers over its young, that spreads its wings to catch them and carries them on its pinions. The LORD alone led him; no foreign god was with him. He made him ride on the heights of the land and fed

him with the fruit of the fields. He nourished him with honey from the rock, and with oil from the flinty crag, with curds and milk from herd and flock and with fattened lambs and goats, with choice rams of Bashan and the finest kernels of wheat. You drank the foaming blood of the grape.
Deuteronomy 32:7-14 (NIV)

Oh, how we hear the **love and concern** that God had for these people. ***He shielded him and guarded him as the "apple of His eye."*** God loved them so much that they were protected by him and were considered a most precious thing to him.

On the day you were born your umbilical cord was not cut, you weren't bathed and cleaned up, you weren't rubbed with salt, you weren't wrapped in a baby blanket. No one cared a fig for you. No one did one thing to care for you tenderly in these ways. You were thrown out into a vacant lot and left there, dirty and unwashed—a newborn nobody wanted. "'And then I came by. I saw you all miserable and bloody. Yes, I said to you, lying there helpless and filthy, "Live! Grow up like a plant in the field!" And you did. You grew up. You grew tall and matured as a woman, full-breasted, with flowing hair. But you were naked and vulnerable, fragile and exposed. "'I came by again and saw you, saw that you were ready for love and a lover. I took care of you, dressed you and protected you. I promised you my love and entered the covenant of marriage with you. I, God, the Master, gave my word. You became mine. I gave you a good bath, washing off all that old blood, and anointed you with aromatic oils. I dressed you in a colorful gown and put leather sandals on your feet. I gave you linen blouses and a fashionable wardrobe of expensive clothing. I adorned you with jewelry: I placed bracelets on your wrists, fitted you out with a necklace, emerald rings, sapphire earrings, and a diamond tiara. You were provided with everything precious and beautiful: with exquisite clothes and elegant food, garnished with honey and oil. You were absolutely stunning. You were a queen! You became world-famous, a legendary beauty brought to perfection by my adornments. Decree of God, the Master.
Ezekiel 16: 4-14 (The Message)

Oh, what intimacy and love was shown in supplying their **physical blessings**! At a season in our relationship, my husband used to go out and buy me shoes and dresses of his choosing. It has been some time since he has done that for me.

It is not because he doesn't desire to do this for me anymore, but there just isn't much to choose from where we live at this time. Just the other day he mentioned how much he enjoyed doing that for me and he missed it. It dawned on me that this was such an expression of his love for me. I pray that I always recognize how much he really does love me and not take it for granted.

> *I will mention the lovingkindnesses of the LORD and the praises of the LORD, according to all that the LORD has bestowed on us, and the great goodness toward the house of Israel, which He has bestowed on them according to His mercies, according to the multitude of His lovingkindnesses. For He said, "Surely they are My people, children who will not lie." So He became their Savior. In all their affliction He was afflicted, and the Angel of His Presence saved them; in His love and in His pity He redeemed them; and He bore them and carried them all the days of old.*
> *Isaiah 63: 7-9 (NIV)*

Can you hear how God, the Almighty, the Creator of the universe loved them so much that when they hurt, He hurt? Can you hear how He suffered right along with them when they got into trouble? Some 4,000 years later we read that Jesus Christ, our High Priest was also, *"touched with the feelings of our infirmities"* Hebrews 4:15 (KJV). **God cared about their sufferings.**

Yes, God's intention was that we look to the "Church in the Wilderness" as an example of His intention for covenant love relationship. And in doing so, we witnessed his love and concern, his desire for intimacy; and his physical provision. All this was solid evidence of His love and that he cared about their trials and their suffering. Yet there is still so much more.

Chapter Two

Looking to Israel, Our Example

Central Theme
God intended for us, the "New Testament Church", to look to the "Church in the Wilderness" as an example or a pattern (in some aspects) for the church of today.

If we, as the New Testament Church, will look back and study or examine the love relationship that the Father had with Israel, it will give us a greater understanding of the love He intends to have with us. God had a love covenant relationship with the nation of Israel and He has not changed in dealing with His people. In looking back to how he interacted with Israel, we witnessed his love and concern, his desire for intimacy, and his physical provision. All this was solid evidence of His love for them and that He cared about their trials and their suffering.

1. Read 1 Corinthians 10: 1-14 at least five times before answering the questions that are to follow.

2. What is God saying concerning the nation of Israel and the New Testament Church?

_____

_____

_____

_____

_____

3. Look up the word "example" and write down the definition.

_____

_____

_____

_____

_____

4. Now read Deuteronomy 7: 1-10 at least five times.

5. Why did God choose Israel to be a holy people unto Himself?

_____

_____

_____

_____

_____

_____

6. What was the promise to that nation in verse 9?

_____

_____

_____

_____

_____

_____

7. Read Deuteronomy 32: 7-14 and Ezekiel 16: 4-14. Now write in your own words how God showed His love for Israel.

_____

_____

_____

_____

_____

_____

_____

_____

_____

_____

_____

_____

_____

_____

APPLICATION...

8. I read somewhere that not to believe is not to accept. If this is true, then to believe is to accept. If you believe that it is God's desire to enter into a love covenant relationship with you, then write a confession of faith of the fact.

_____

_____

_____

_____

_____

9. Now write down at least ten things that God has blessed you with that serve as proof of His supplying your physical blessings.

_____

_____

_____

_____

_____

_____

_____

_____

_____

_____

_____

_____

10. Now write down at least one trial that you went through and you know that you know that it was God who brought you through that trial.

_____

_____

_____

_____

_____

_____

_____

_____

_____

_____

_____

_____

_____

11. Do you now believe that it is the will of the Father to love you and, if so, why?

_____

_____

_____

_____

_____

_____

_____

_____

12. Do you feel that you are worthy to accept His love? Please explain your answer.

_____

_____

_____

_____

_____

_____

_____

_____

God is no respecter of persons and He loves us all the same. I remember the day that God revealed to me that the ground at the foot of the cross was level. Let me explain… Every person on the planet was at one time or is a sinner and all are in need of a Savior and all have to come to Christ. From the poorest to the richest-it is all the same. God does not love one more than the other. It was at that moment that I saw my worth in God and knew that it did not matter where I had come from or how I was raised or what I had been through or hadn't had in life. The only thing that mattered was that I was loved by the Father and He saw me as His child and offered me no more or less that anyone else. He loved me for who I was and I did not have to change myself or make myself good enough to be accepted by Him.

All I had to do was accept His invitation to come!

Prayer

Father, thank you so much for loving me. Please help me to really accept the fact that you chose me simply because you loved me and ordained me to be your child. In Jesus Name, Amen.

JOURNALING

(Now write down those things that come to your mind as you reflect upon this lesson. It may help to go back over the questions and the responses.)

_____

_____

_____

_____

_____

_____

_____

_____

_____

_____

_____

_____

_____

_____

_____

_____

_____

_____

_____

_____

_____

_____

_____

_____

_____

_____

_____

_____

_____

_____

_____

_____

_____

_____

_____

_____

_____

_____

_____

_____

_____

_____

_____

_____

_____

_____

_____

Embracing the Love of the Father:
Israel, a Peculiar Treasure

In the third month after the children of Israel had gone out of the land of
Egypt, on the same day, they came to the Wilderness of Sinai. For they had
departed from Rephidim, had come to the Wilderness of Sinai, and camped
in the wilderness. So Israel camped there before the mountain. And Moses
went up to God, and the LORD called to him from the mountain, saying,
"Thus you shall say to the house of Jacob, and tell the children of Israel:
'You have seen what I did to the Egyptians, and how I bore you on eagles'
wings and brought you to Myself. Now therefore, if you will indeed obey
My voice and keep My covenant, then you shall be a special treasure to Me
above all people; for all the earth is Mine. And you shall be to Me a king-
dom of priests and a holy nation.' These are the words which you shall
speak to the children of Israel."
Exodus 19: 1-6

In Exodus the 19th chapter, verses one through six, the Lord told the nation of
Israel that He bore them on eagle's wings. In the natural when it is time for the
young eagle to leave its nest; the mother eagle must prepare that eagle to leave
that nest. The first thing she does is to make the nest, which had been a place of
comfort, become very uncomfortable. The mother eagle does this by stirring up
that nest. She removes the softness and breaks twigs so that the jagged ends
stick out. God did the same thing to His nation in that he allowed conditions in
Egypt to become so unbearable that the people began to cry out to him. The
mother eagle will also begin fluttering over her eaglet beating him with her
wings. To escape this fluttering the eaglet will move to the very edge of the nest,
at which time the mother eagle will spread out her wings. The eaglet will get on
her back and hold on, soaring with that mother; going wherever she goes. Thus
begins the process of the eaglet learning how to fly on his own.

God had brought His nation out of the land of Egypt caring for her every step of the way as they entered into the wilderness of Sinai. It would be there that He would give them a cloud by day and a fire by night to lead them where He would have them to go, just as the eaglet did, holding on to its mother's back as she soared. So would the children of Israel follow the Father.

When the Lord called to Moses from the mountain, He told him to tell the people that if they would continue to walk in covenant with him that they would be a **peculiar treasure** unto Him above all people. The word peculiar in the Hebrew is hllgs and it means possession, property, valued treasure. The people of Israel belonged to God. That meant He alone was responsible for their well-being, for supplying all of their needs, and for protecting them from all hurt and harm and danger. God likened Israel to treasure. A treasure is something considered of great value or worth. A treasure is something of usefulness as opposed to uselessness. The nation of Israel was to be a people esteemed as rare or precious. They were to be a people of great purpose.

> *For the LORD has chosen Jacob for Himself, Israel for His special treasure.*
> *Psalm 135:4*

> *For you are a holy people to the LORD your God, and the LORD has chosen you to be a people for Himself, a special treasure above all the peoples who are on the face of the earth.*
> *Deuteronomy 14:2*

> *Today you have proclaimed the LORD to be your God, and that you will walk in His ways and keep His statutes, His commandments, and His judgments, and that you will obey His voice. Also today the LORD has proclaimed you to be His special people, just as He promised you, that you should keep all His commandments, and that He will set you high above all nations which He has made, in praise, in name, and in honor, and that you may be a holy people to the LORD your God, just as He has spoken."*
> *Deuteronomy 26:17-19*

It is so evident from the Scriptures that Israel was specifically chosen by the Father and that they held a special place in His heart. Their relationship was one of uniqueness. It was unique because they were the fewest of all people and the most unlikely to be chosen and yet God chose them for His kingdom purpose and valued them as so precious that He alone would be responsible for their care and protection. They were His peculiar treasure, but also a kingdom of priests.

Chapter Three

Israel, a Peculiar Treasure

Central Theme
The relationship that the Father had with Israel was one of uniqueness. They were His peculiar treasure.

Israel, a nation in bondage, cried out to the Father for deliverance and He did indeed send them a deliverer. He proved His love to them over and over again by His divine providence for them. The nation held such a special place in His heart. He chose them because He loved them and their relationship was indeed a unique one. They were His peculiar treasure. He alone would be responsible for their complete well being.

1. Read Exodus Chapters one through nineteen before answering the questions that follow.

2. From before the start of the Exodus until their arrival at Mount Sinai, list at least ten ways that you read God providing for Israel, thus proving that the nation held a special place in the Father's heart.

_____

_____

_____

_____

_____

_____

_____

_____

_____

_____

_____

_____

3. In verse 4 of Exodus chapter nineteen the Lord said that He "bore them on eagles' wings and brought them to Himself. Write in your own words, an analogy between how a mother eagle cares for her eaglet and how the Father cared for Israel.

_____

_____

_____

_____
_____
_____
_____
_____
_____

4. Look up the words "peculiar" and "treasure" in a dictionary and write their meanings below.

_____
_____
_____
_____
_____
_____
_____
_____

5. How was Israel a peculiar treasure unto the Father?

_____
_____
_____
_____
_____
_____
_____

6. Read Psalm 139 in its entirety at least five times. Read it aloud at least once.

7. Now go back and re-read verses 13 through 18. What do these verses mean to you personally?

_____

_____

_____

_____

_____

8. Now read Jeremiah 1: 1-5. Do you believe that just as God chose Jeremiah before he was born, that you also were chosen by the Father? How does this make you feel?

_____

_____

_____

_____

_____

9. Why do you think that He chose you?

_____

_____

_____

_____

_____

APPLICATION

10. Write down a confession of faith concerning your position or standing with God. Read it aloud to yourself.

_____

_____

_____

_____

_____

_____

Just as Israel was specifically chosen by the Father and held a special place in His heart so do we. Theirs was a unique relationship in that they were the fewest of all people and the most unlikely to be chosen. Yet God chose them for His kingdom purpose and valued them as so precious that He alone would be responsible for their care and protection.

Prayer...

Father, thank you so much for choosing me; before I was even born. Please help me to understand my position in you and to accept my position in you. Help me to realize that you have chosen to be responsible for my care and well being and that I am to trust you for everything. In Jesus Name, Amen.

JOURNALING

(Now write down those things that come to your mind as you reflect upon this lesson. It may help to go back over the questions and the responses.)

_____

_____

_____

_____

_____

_____

_____

_____

_____

_____

_____

_____

_____

_____

_____

_____

_____

_____

_____

_____

Embracing the Love of the Father:
Israel, a Kingdom of Priests

*You have seen what I did to the Egyptians and how I bore you on eagles'
wings and brought you to Myself. Now therefore, if you will indeed obey My
voice and keep My covenant, then you shall be a special treasure to Me above
all people; for all the earth is Mine. And you shall be to Me a kingdom of
priests and a holy nation.' These are the words which you shall speak to the
children of Israel." So Moses came and called for the elders of the people, and
laid before them all these words which the LORD commanded him. Then all
the people answered together and said, "All that the LORD has spoken we
will do." So Moses brought back the words of the people to the LORD.*
Exodus 19: 4-8

The word priest is used some 700 times in the Old Testament; however, it is not
always in relationship to the entire nation of Israel representing God as priests.
Walter B. Shurden in his book, The Doctrine of the Priesthood of Believers,
says, "A priest is someone who relates to and acts for God. The Hebrew word
for priest is kohen, a noun, and it is associated with the verb kahen, which in all
probability means to stand. So, then a priest is one who stood before God as a
servant or minister." To help us better understand this concept of the entire nation of Israel being a kingdom of priests; let's go back to the time when they
were released from Egyptian bondage.

God miraculously had delivered the children of Israel out of Egyptian bondage.
As the Egyptian army chased them down, God literally opened up the waters of
the Red Sea and the entire nation walked over on dry land. Almost immediately
they went into the wilderness of Shur and after being there for three days they
found no water. They finally came to a place called Marah and the water there
was bitter --it was undrinkable. God performed another miracle and the waters

became sweet or drinkable. It was there in Marah that the Lord told them that if they would obey his commandments, he would put none of the diseases upon them that he had brought upon the Egyptians. He revealed himself to them as Jehovah Rapha, the Lord Who heals you.

They journeyed onward and came to a place called Elim and in Elim there were 12 wells of water and 70 palm trees. It was there that they camped, close to this water source. The name Elim meant trees and they stayed there for about a month. From there they journeyed to the Wilderness of Sin. It was there that God miraculously provided food for them and they feasted on that miraculous provision for 40 years.

The nation had thus far journeyed from Egypt (their place of bondage) to Marah (place where what was bitter was turned into sweet) to Elim (a place of miraculous protection and provision) to the Wilderness of Sin (a place between Elim and Mount Sinai) to a place called Rephidim (its name meant rest but it became a place of war). It was in Rephidim that they fought their first battle and God revealed Himself to them as Jehovah Nissi --The Lord Is My Banner.

They traveled on and we find them in the Wilderness of Sinai ready to camp before the mountain of God. Before they got settled in God, who already had revealed himself to them as the One who loved them, their provider, protector and guide, desired to seal their relationship with a covenant agreement. Let's read what happened in Exodus 19: 3-6.

> *And Moses went up to God, and the LORD called to him from the mountain, saying, "Thus you shall say to the house of Jacob, and tell the children of Israel: 'You have seen what I did to the Egyptians, and how I bore you on eagles' wings and brought you to Myself. Now therefore, if you will indeed obey My voice and keep My covenant, then you shall be a special treasure to Me above all people; for all the earth is Mine. And you shall be to Me a kingdom of priests and a holy nation.' These are the words which you shall speak to the children of Israel."*

God extended an invitation to that entire nation to become priests, to become a people who would stand before Him as His servants or ministers. They would relate to the Father and they would act for Him.

So Moses came and called for the elders of the people, and laid before
them all these words which the LORD commanded him. Then all the people
answered together and said, "All that the LORD has spoken we will do."
So Moses brought back the words of the people to the LORD.
Exodus 19:7-8

In their response to the Father, that day they agreed to be His kingdom, under His sovereign rule. They would reign with their King, God Jehovah!

Strangers shall stand and feed your flocks, and the sons of the foreigner
shall be your plowmen and your vinedressers. But you shall be named the
priests of the LORD, they shall call you the servants of our God. You shall
eat the riches of the Gentiles, and in their glory you shall boast.
Isaiah 61: 5-6

God's original intent was that Israel would be a kingdom of priests. Oh, they had the formal priesthood as well and we can learn much from the divine order of the Levitical Priesthood. There is much symbolism in the priesthood that can help us to better understand what it meant to God that the nation of Israel would be a corporate kingdom of priests. We first must ask and attempt to answer the question: "How important are symbols to a group of people or a nation?"

Some years ago I was asked to deliver a message to a group of women and the theme was "America's Godly Heritage". One of the things that I put emphasis on was our nation's flag and how a nation's flag is its symbol of unity or solidarity. That is why the flag was always taken into battle. During the message I went into the very design of the original flag and made speculations and compared those speculations with the Word of God. The end result was that we all looked at the American Flag quite differently than we had before and it gave us greater meaning of the Scripture, "*Blessed is the nation whose God is the Lord*" Psalm 33: 12.

When Moses went up Mount Sinai and there spent 40 days and nights, the Lord gave him the specifications for the Levitical Priesthood. If we look closely, it is in the symbolism of the Levitical Priesthood that we can find what it means to be a kingdom of priests for the entire nation.

So I will consecrate the tabernacle of meeting and the altar. I will also consecrate both Aaron and his sons to minister to Me as priests. I will dwell among the children of Israel and will be their God. And they shall know that I am the LORD their God, who brought them up out of the land of Egypt, that I may dwell among them. I am the LORD their God.
Exodus 29: 44-46

We see two things symbolized in this verse of Scripture that point to the priesthood of the entire nation. First we see God's divine deliverance of the nation from Egypt. The fact that God made a way for his chosen people to finally come out of Egyptian bondage represented or symbolized His divine intervention. God did not intervene because they were a great nation, nor had they done anything to deserve it. Quite the contrary. Simply because He loved them He had chosen them, and He had chosen them simply because He loved them.

The selecting of Aaron and his sons for the Levitical priesthood was God's sovereign choice. The choosing and the deliverance were both acts of grace-nothing more, nothing less. The deliverance became a constant reminder of God's intervention in their everyday lives, and the choosing of those for the priesthood became a constant reminder that God chooses whom He will.

Thousands of years later the Apostle Peter wrote concerning us… *But you are a chosen generation, a royal priesthood, a holy nation, His own special people, that you may proclaim the praises of Him who called you out of darkness into His marvelous light." 1 Peter 2:9* Beloved, you have been hand-picked, chosen by God, and your purpose is to show forth His praises with your life. You were not an accident. God chose you! The Father told Jeremiah, the prophet, *"Then the word of the LORD came to me, saying: Before I formed you in the womb I knew you; before you were born I sanctified you; I ordained you a prophet to the nations." Jeremiah 1: 5*

The second thing symbolized in the Levitical Priesthood is the dwelling place of the Father, The Tabernacle of Meeting. It was the physical place where the presence of God would be manifest to His people. It was where the priest would minister, for they were the ones appointed by God to take care of this, His dwelling place. They were the caretakers. Walter B. Shurden says that this was God's evidence of His presence in their midst. The nation was constantly aware of the presence of God in their midst and the priests were the living witnesses of His presence.

Therefore, laying aside all malice, all deceit, hypocrisy, envy, and all evil speaking, as newborn babes, desire the pure milk of the word, that you may grow thereby, if indeed you have tasted that the Lord is gracious. Coming to Him as to a living stone, rejected indeed by men, but chosen by God and precious, you also, as living stones, are being built up a spiritual house, a holy priesthood, to offer up spiritual sacrifices acceptable to God through Jesus Christ. Therefore it is also contained in the Scripture, "Behold, I lay in Zion a chief cornerstone, elect, precious, and he who believes on Him will by no means be put to shame." Therefore, to you who believe, He is precious; but to those who are disobedient, "The stone which the builders rejected has become the chief cornerstone," and "A stone of stumbling and a rock of offense." They stumble, being disobedient to the word, to which they also were appointed. But you are a chosen generation, a royal priest-hood, a holy nation, His own special people, that you may proclaim the praises of Him who called you out of darkness into His marvelous light...
1 Peter 2: 1-9

Just as the Tabernacle of Meeting was the place where the presence of God was manifested, and the Levitical Priests were the caretakers of that dwelling place for the Father, we are now that spiritual house. We are that building with Christ being the Chief Cornerstone. We are that building not created with the hands of man, but custom built by the Father, purchased by the Son, and inhabited by the Holy Spirit which is the Spirit of Christ.

For through Him we both have access by one Spirit to the Father. Now, therefore, you are no longer strangers and foreigners, but fellow citizens with the saints and members of the household of God, having been built on the foundation of the apostles and prophets, Jesus Christ Himself being the chief cornerstone, in whom the whole building, being fitted together, grows into a holy temple in the Lord, in whom you also are being built together for a dwelling place of God in the Spirit.
Ephesians 2: 18-22

We were chosen by God to be built into a dwelling place for Himself. Just think that a Holy God could choose such an unholy, unworthy vessel to be a habitati-on for Himself. Yet I believe that was His very purpose to keep us humble and dependent upon Him. Oh, the mercy and grace of such a wonderful and kind-hearted and loving Father. Oh, how He loves us and desires us to embrace that love. Still there is more. We are a holy nation.

Chapter Four

Israel, a Kingdom of Priests

Central Theme
**God chose Israel to be an example
of the priesthood.**

God extended an invitation to the entire nation of Israel to become priests, to become a people who would stand before Him as His servants as ministers. They would relate to the Father and would act on His behalf.

1. Walter B. Shurden in his book, <u>The Doctrine of the Priesthood of Believers</u>, gives a definition of a priest. Write that definition below.

_____

_____

_____

_____

_____

2. Where in the Scriptures can you find the invitation that God extended to Israel to stand before Him as a people who would serve as His servants or ministers?

_____

_____

_____

_____

_____

_____

3. What symbolism in the formal Levitical priesthood helps us to understand how Israel would be a corporate kingdom of priests? See Exodus 29: 44-46.

_____

_____

_____

_____

_____

_____

_____

_____

_____

_____

4. When God saves us we are brought out of bondage just as Israel was brought out of Egyptian bondage. Write a brief testimony of how God saved you and brought you out of bondage.

_____

_____

_____

_____

_____

_____

_____

_____

_____

_____

_____

5. We are now the dwelling place of the Spirit of God. How does it make you feel to know that the same Spirit that raised Christ from the dead dwells on the inside of you?

_____

_____

_____

APPLICATION

6. List at least three ways that you intend to be become better in your service to the Lord and how you intend to accomplish this.

_____

_____

_____

_____

_____

_____

_____

_____

When we were living in sin and doing things our own way, God divinely intervened and wooed us by His Holy Spirit into a love relationship with Him that shall last throughout eternity. We are now His house where His Spirit abides and we are caretakers of that house. We relate to the Father and we act for Him. May people see our good works and it bring glory to the Father.

Prayer

Lord, as I humbly present myself and my service before you I ask that you would show me areas where I am in need of improvement. Father, show me where I am lacking and then help me to be the best me that I can be in my service for you. Give me the true heart of a servant. Please examine my heart and correct me in those things that would prevent me from being effective for you. Teach me as you did the disciples how to be a true servant. In Jesus Name, Amen.

JOURNALING

(Now write down those things that come to your mind as you reflect upon this lesson. It may help to go back over the questions and the responses.)

_____

_____

_____

_____

_____

_____

_____

_____

_____

_____

_____

_____

_____

_____

_____

_____

_____

_____

_____

_____

_____

_____

_____

_____

_____

_____

Embracing the Love of the Father:
Israel, a Holy Nation

You have seen what I did to the Egyptians, and how I bore you on eagles'
wings and brought you to Myself. Now therefore, if you will indeed obey
My voice and keep My covenant, then you shall be a special treasure to Me
above all people; for all the earth is Mine. And you shall be to Me a king-
*dom of priests and a **holy nation.** ' These are the words which you shall*
speak to the children of Israel."
Exodus 19: 4-6

From the time we are born we are constantly being programmed. It is as if we are human computers downloading information constantly and storing that information on the hard drives of our souls to be recalled at a later date. I was saved at the crusade of a charismatic preacher and soon thereafter joined a very prominent Pentecostal denomination. This was during the early 80's so there were still some in the church who felt that holiness (for women) was not cutting your hair, not wearing make-up, and not wearing pants. For whatever reason, I never got caught up in all the denominational "thou shall not" traditional rules and regulations. All I knew was that God loved me and I loved Him and I wanted to serve him for the rest of my life. I found it so interesting, though, that the ones who claimed to be the holiest from their outward appearance proved at times to be the biggest devils! I guess you could say that I became aware early on that holiness had less to do with outward appearance than the condition of the heart.

God called Israel, "a holy nation." To try to understand what God meant I believe we must first start with God Himself. His character is holiness.

*"Who is like You, O LORD, among the gods? Who is like You, glorious in
holiness, fearful in praises, doing wonders?
Exodus 15:11*

*"No one is holy like the LORD, For there is none besides You, Nor is there
any rock like our God.
1 Samuel 2:2*

*To whom then will you liken Me, Or to whom shall I be equal?" says the
Holy One.
Isaiah 40:25*

*For thus says the High and Lofty One who inhabits eternity, whose name is
Holy: I dwell in the high and holy place, with him who has a contrite and
humble spirit, to revive the spirit of the humble, and to revive the heart of
the contrite ones.
Isaiah 57:15*

God is holy. The definition for holy as it pertains to God is worthy of worship,
exalted, or worthy of complete devotion for He is perfect in goodness and righteousness. God is unique in that there is no one else like Him. It is possible that
by calling Israel a holy nation, God was saying that they were:

- Unique in their relationship with him. Holiness means to be consecrated
  to God and to be set apart for his will and his purpose. This fact is what
  made the nation of Israel unique. They were not like any other nation.

*For you are a holy people to the LORD your God; the LORD your God has
chosen you to be a people for Himself, a special treasure above all the
peoples on the face of the earth.
Deuteronomy 7:6*

- A holy nation, meaning that they belonged to God and He belonged to them. Their dependence was solely on Him, neither upon themselves nor anyone else but God.

- A holy nation in that God expected them to be obedient to Him, and that through this obedience He would bless them tremendously.

Then it shall come to pass, because you listen to these judgments, and keep and do them, that the LORD your God will keep with you the covenant and the mercy which He swore to your fathers. And He will love you and bless you and multiply you; He will also bless the fruit of your womb and the fruit of your land, your grain and your new wine and your oil, the increase of your cattle and the offspring of your flock, in the land of which He swore to your fathers to give you. You shall be blessed above all peoples; there shall not be a male or female barren among you or among your livestock. And the LORD will take away from you all sickness, and will afflict you with none of the terrible diseases of Egypt which you have known, but will lay them on all those who hate you. 1Also you shall destroy all the peoples whom the LORD your God delivers over to you; your eye shall have no pity on them; nor shall you serve their gods, for that will be a snare to you. "If you should say in your heart, 'These nations are greater than I; how can I dispossess them?'— you shall not be afraid of them, but you shall remember well what the LORD your God did to Pharaoh and to all Egypt: the great trials which your eyes saw, the signs and the wonders, the mighty hand and the outstretched arm, by which the LORD your God brought you out. So shall the LORD your God do to all the peoples of whom you are afraid. Moreover the LORD your God will send the hornet among them until those who are left, who hide themselves from you, are destroyed. You shall not be terrified of them; for the LORD your God, the great and awesome God, is among you. And the LORD your God will drive out those nations before you little by little; you will be unable to destroy them at once, lest the beasts of the field become too numerous for you. But the LORD your God will deliver them over to you, and will inflict defeat upon them until they are destroyed. And He will deliver their kings into your hand, and you will destroy their name from under heaven; no one shall be able to stand against you until you have destroyed them. You shall burn the carved images of their gods with fire; you shall not covet the silver or gold that is on them, nor take it for yourselves, lest you be snared by it; for it is an abomination to the LORD your God. Nor shall you bring an abomination into your house, lest you be doomed to destruction like it. You shall utterly detest it and utterly abhor it, for it is an accursed thing.
Deuteronomy 7: 12-26

"Now it shall come to pass, if you diligently obey the voice of the LORD your God, to observe carefully all His commandments which I command you today, that the LORD your God will set you high above all nations of the earth. And all these blessings shall come upon you and overtake you, because you obey the voice of the LORD your God:" Blessed shall you be in the city, and blessed shall you be in the country. "Blessed shall be the fruit of your body, the produce of your ground and the increase of your herds, the increase of your cattle and the offspring of your flocks. "Blessed shall be your basket and your kneading bowl. "Blessed shall you be when you come in, and blessed shall you be when you go out. "The LORD will cause your enemies who rise against you to be defeated before your face; they shall come out against you one way and flee before you seven ways." The LORD will command the blessing on you in your storehouses and in all to which you set your hand, and He will bless you in the land which the LORD your God is giving you. "The LORD will establish you as a holy people to Himself, just as He has sworn to you, if you keep the commandments of the LORD your God and walk in His ways. Then all peoples of the earth shall see that you are called by the name of the LORD, and they shall be afraid of you. And the LORD will grant you plenty of goods, in the fruit of your body, in the increase of your livestock, and in the produce of your ground, in the land of which the LORD swore to your fathers to give you. The LORD will open to you His good treasure, the heavens, to give the rain to your land in its season, and to bless all the work of your hand. You shall lend to many nations, but you shall not borrow. And the LORD will make you the head and not the tail; you shall be above only, and not be beneath, if you heed the commandments of the LORD your God, which I command you today, and are careful to observe them. So you shall not turn aside from any of the words which I command you this day, to the right or the left, to go after other gods to serve them.
Deuteronomy 28: 1-14

What does this mean for us today? God has not changed. He is still a holy God and all believers are His holy people.

But as He who called you is holy, you also be holy in all your conduct, 16 because it is written, "Be holy, for I am holy."
1 Peter 1: 15-16

But you are a chosen generation, a royal priesthood, a holy nation, His own special people, that you may proclaim the praises of Him who called you out of darkness into His marvelous light; who once were not a people but are now the people of God, who had not obtained mercy but now have obtained mercy.
1 Peter 2: 9-10

- **Holy nation means that we are unique in our relationship with God** … God chose us. He consecrated us to be His people, the sheep of His pasture. We serve a holy God who is worthy of our worship and reverence towards Him, and because we reverence Him we are obedient to Him. Instead of our relationship with the Father being one of religion it is one of love.

- **Holy nation means that we belong to the Father** … Jesus said, "Apart from the Father I can do nothing." That, too, is our stand. Our dependence is totally upon Him because we belong to Him and Him to us.

- **Holy nation means that we are obedient to the Father**…. We serve a holy God who is worthy of our worship and reverence towards Him and because we reverence Him we are obedient to Him.

Israel gave us an example of what it means to be a holy nation unto God. In His unique relationship with this nation we see clearly our own relationship --one of knowing that we are loved by a Holy Father who has chosen us for Himself. Out of that love relationship comes reverence for him and out of reverence for him comes obedience to him. Yet there is more. Let's explore; we are the apple of His eye!

Chapter Five

Israel, a Holy Nation

Central Theme
God called Israel to be a holy nation. We, too, are that Holy nation.

God is holy and He has holy love for His holy nation. God called Israel to be that holy nation unto Himself. They were unique in their relationship with him in that they belonged to him and he belonged to them. He expected them to be obedient and through their obedience he would bless them.

1. To the best of your ability, explain the holiness of God.

_____

_____

_____

_____

_____

2. How is God's holiness a reflection of His love?

_____

_____

_____

_____

_____

3. Explain three ways in which Israel was called a holy nation unto God.

_____

_____

_____

_____

_____

_____

_____

_____

_____

4. Now explain how these same three things apply to the New Testament church.

_____

_____

_____

_____

_____

_____

_____

_____

_____

_____

_____

_____

_____

5. Read the entire 7th and 28th chapters of Deuteronomy.

6. What does holiness have to do with a person's conduct?

_____

_____

_____

_____

_____

_____

7. Read 1 Peter 2: 9-10. Expound on this passage of Scripture in your own words.

_____

_____

_____

_____

_____

_____

_____

8. What would you say obedience has to do with holiness?

_____

_____

_____

_____

_____

9. How does it make you feel to know that you have been declared holy by the Father?

_____

_____

_____

_____

_____

_____

APPLICATION

10. How do you intend to pursue holiness in your conduct? Remember it starts in the heart.

_____

_____

_____

11. Write a confession of faith concerning your position of holiness in the Father.

_____

_____

_____

_____

Israel gave us an example of what it means to be a holy nation unto the Lord. And in the example that they set before us we can only deduce that because God is a holy God and that He chose us to be his own; He has declared that we are holy as well. May we always strive to live up to what God has already declared that we are.

Prayer

My most gracious and Holy Heavenly Father, I thank you that I have been declared holy by you because of the blood of your Son Jesus. I thank you that holiness is a condition of my heart. I ask that you continually work on my heart so that my actions would be pleasing to you and that they would truly reflect your glory. In Jesus Name, Amen.

JOURNALING

(Now write down those things that come to your mind as you reflect upon this lesson. It may help to go back over the questions and the responses.)

_____

_____

_____

_____

_____

_____

_____

_____

_____

_____

_____

_____

_____

_____

_____

_____

_____

_____

_____

_____

_____

_____

_____

_____

Embracing the Love of the Father: Israel, the Apple of His Eye

He found him in a desert land and in the wasteland, a howling wilderness;
He encircled him, He instructed him, He kept him as the apple of His eye.
Deuteronomy 32:10

Up to this point I have stated that it is God's will for us that we not just recognize that He loves us, but also that we allow Him to cultivate in us a deep understanding of His love which will lead us to accept and truly embrace the love so freely given. We have looked at Israel as an example of the love of the Father being lavished upon a people, not because they deserved it but simply because they were chosen by Him. We've learned that in His love for them He appointed them as His peculiar treasure. They had a special place in the heart of the Father and because they did he would be responsible for their complete care and protection. We further learned that in His love for them He invited them to become a kingdom of priests. That invitation went beyond the formal Levitical Priesthood; it was a corporate call to relate to the Father and to act for Him. Finally, but not least, we saw that in the Father's love for Israel He declared them a holy nation unto Himself, which meant that they were unique in their relationship with Him. It meant that they belonged to Him. It meant that He belonged to them. It meant that He expected their total loyalty and obedience and that through their obedience to Him that He would bless them.

In Deuteronomy 32: 10 the Lord also said that He kept Israel, His beloved, his chosen people as, *"the apple of His eye."* It is a term that is synonymous with the nation of Israel and speaks volumes of the love and care that God had for this nation. So let's examine how the Lord made His love for Israel so evident in keeping them as the apple of His eye. We will see how it applies to us today.

When studying this verse of Scripture the Lord spoke to me so simply and this is what He revealed to me.

I had been invited to speak at the Hessen Area Protestant Women of the Chapel Spring Rally. I was absolutely elated as I have a heart for the women of PWOC and it had been many years since I'd had the opportunity to fellowship with this group of precious ladies. It was during the preparation of my outline for the sessions that I felt the nudging of the Lord as He directed me to Psalm 17:8 -"*Keep me as the apple of Your eye, hide me under the shadow of Your wings ...*" I read the verse and then read it again. It was then that I hear the voice of my Father say to me, "You are one of my apple girls." I must say that I chuckled. As I began to meditate on the Scripture and study, here are just some of the things that I gleaned.

Psalm 17 was a prayer that David prayed to the Father. He started his prayer by saying, "*Hear a just cause, O Lord, attend to my cry; give ear to my prayer which is not from deceitful lips.*" Can you picture the man, David, the psalmist and worshipper perhaps kneeling before His heavenly Father asking to be heard, at the same time knowing that he would be heard? David went before God openly and sincerely. Then he said, "*Let my vindication come from your presence; let your eyes look on the things that are upright. You have tested my heart; you have visited me in the night; you have tried me and found nothing; I have purposed that my mouth shall not transgress. I have called upon you for you will hear me, O God; incline your ear to me, and hear my speech. Show your marvelous loving-kindness by your right hand, O you who save those who trust in you from those who rise up against them.*" And finally in verse 8 he says, "*Keep me as the **apple of your eye**; hide me under the shadow of your wings...*" David was asking the Father for His protection from his enemies. Oh, how many times have I personally entreated the Lord for His protection? You know; He has always provided.

David asked the Lord to protect him, but to what extent? I believe the clue can be found in five little words, "*as the apple of His eye.*" The word "apple" in the Hebrew is 'iyshowm (pronounced ee-shone) and is translated as the "little man of the eye." The little man of the eye, supposedly, means the reflection of someone seen in the pupil of the eye. There are two trains of thought here.

The first thought is that the pupil is a vital part of the entire eye. The entire eye is a symbol of well thought-out protection. You see, God designed the eye to sit back into the eye socket. If it protruded outside of the socket it stands to reason that it would be more susceptible to injury. The pupil of the eye is protected by a clear transparent dome called the cornea, and is protected by the eyelid whose function of blinking helps keep the eye clean and moist. It is further protected by eyelashes to help keep dust and dirt and other unwanted things out. The pupil is extremely well protected, fortified even, so that it can function the way God designed it to.

The second thought is that of the pupil being the "little man of the eye". That means it is the one's reflection seen in the pupil. When you look into the pupil of another you will see your own reflection. When I look into the eyes of the Father, He is also looking back at me and what I see in His eyes is how He sees me. Oh, beloved how distorted is our view of ourselves as it has been shaped by so many outside influences. We've been told all our lives what we should look like in accordance with the standards of the world. The image that we have of ourselves has become so distorted that it will take the love of the Father to convince us that He sees us so differently than how we see ourselves. Oh Father, please correct our vision. Please cause us to see ourselves as you see us. Cause us to see ourselves as your "apple gals."

Recently I was having dinner with my church family and I shared the aforementioned with the group. One of the brothers asked me, "How do we focus and look into the eyes of the Father in order to see ourselves reflected?" Without even giving it a thought I said, "By looking in His word." The conversation continued. When I got home later that night I questioned the Lord about my answer to my brother and He reminded me of an incident in my life that had occurred some years before. My family and I were in the United States Army and had been transferred from Hawaii to Fort Devens, Massachusetts. We were waiting to be assigned housing on the post and were living in an apartment a few minutes walk from our church. It just so happened that some missionaries from Ireland were coming into town and our pastor really needed a decent vehicle to transport them. My husband at the time was on temporary duty assignment attending school in Arizona. I felt that the Lord was speaking to my heart to tell the pastor that they could use our van and that I could carpool to work and the children and I could just walk to church or wherever else we needed to go. After discussing it with Mike I turned over the van to the pastor and never gave it another thought.

Some time later as I was before the Lord, I felt led to read the story of the Good Samaritan. When I got to the part where he placed the man on his own donkey, the Lord stopped me and brought back to my mind how I had obeyed his nudging in allowing the pastor to use our van for those precious missionaries. I still remember as if it were yesterday what my Lord said to me next, "You walked so that others could ride." It humbled me so to hear the Lord tell me something about myself. That day He showed me how that simple act of kindness was a reflection of something that had already been done in His word. Then he further let me know that when I looked into His word I would always see myself reflected there, whether my deeds were good or whether they were bad. The word of God is our mirror and we are to look in it often. That mirror carries the image of the Son. We are constantly and consistently being transformed into His image. We are God's Apple Ladies!

The Psalmist also wrote in Psalms 17:8 -"...*hide me under the shadow of your wings*..." The thought that comes to my mind is that of a mother hen and how she carefully and lovingly gathers her baby chicks under the safety and warmth of her wings, so close to her breast that they can feel and hear her heart beat. In the same way we are the off spring of the Father. We are his daughters and as such He desires to draws us close to Himself, so close as to hear and feel the very beat of his heart.

There we have it --reflection and protection. To be the apple of the Father's eye means that when we look into His eyes, when we are focused upon Him, we will indeed see ourselves as He sees us. We are precious to Him and He will protect us. God will shield us, cover us, guard us, and come to our defense. It is when we are most persecuted that we are protected the most. Now I cannot even get my mind wrapped around that thought, but whether we can immediately grasp it or not, the truth is still the truth. Oh, God, *sanctify us through thy truth; thy word is thy truth! John 17:17* We are God's Apple Ladies!

In Deuteronomy 32:10 the Father speaking of His dealings with Israel said, "*He found him, encircled him, instructed him and kept him as the apple of his eye.*" Now let's explore each of these concepts.

- **He found him**. The nation of Israel had been in Egyptian bondage for forty years and when they cried out to the Lord, He sent a deliverer and brought His people out of bondage. The truth is that God came looking for us. The word of God says that no one can come to him unless they are drawn by His Spirit. We were all lost and needed to be found and rescued from a life of sin. Thank God that He loved us enough to come after us. We are God's Apple Ladies.

- **He encircled him**. To encircle means to completely surround and make secure. To make secure means to protect. God kept his eye upon Israel and, as long as they were obedient to His will, they had victory over every thing and everyone that came against them. When God saved us, He sealed us with His precious Holy Spirit and gave us authority over all the power of the enemy. We can rest safe in the arms of the Father knowing that He protects us and has promised that He will never leave us nor forsake us. Father, protect your apple gals!

- **He instructed him**. After Israel came out of bondage on their way to the Promised Land, the deliverer Moses went up on Mount Carmel and received the Law. The Law was God's instructions to His people for righteous living. God is still instructing us by and through His word. The Psalmist David said, *"Open my eyes Lord that I may behold wondrous things in thy law."* The Father still teaches us His ways as we get into his word and the Spirit of us gives us insight into its meaning. Father, instruct your apple ladies!

- **He kept him**. Kept is the past tense of keep and to keep means to provide with maintenance and support. God so looked after Israel that for forty years their shoes did not even wear out. He also fed them with manna from heaven and water from a rock. They wanted for nothing. The Father sure does know how to take care of what belongs to Him. He is our Provider and makes provision for whatever we have need of. The Lord truly is our Shepherd and we shall not lack. We are God's Apple Ladies!

So, then, to be the apple of the Father's eye means that we are so precious to Him that He tells us who we are. As we look into His eyes we see ourselves as He see us. We are reflectors of His image. To be the apple of the Father's eye means that we have His care and protection. We are His daughters and He sure does know how to completely take care of what belongs to Him. To be the apple of the Father's eye means that as we get into His word He gives us instruction for living a life that will be pleasing to Him.

Thank you, Father, that we have been handpicked by you to serve in your kingdom. We are your beautiful, luscious, and fruitful apple gals! Yet there is still so much more; let's explore. If we are the apple, God has to be the core!

Chapter Six

Israel, The Apple of God's Eye

Central Theme
Just like Israel, we are the "apple of the Father's eye."

Up to this point I have stated that it is God's will for us that we not just recognize that He loves us, but also that we allow Him to cultivate in us a deep understanding of His love which will lead us to accept and truly embrace the love so freely given. We have looked at Israel as an example of the love of the Father being lavished upon a people, not because they deserved it but simply because they were chosen by Him. We've learned that in His love for them He appointed them as His peculiar treasure. They had a special place in the heart of the Father and because they did he would be responsible for their complete care and protection. We further learned that in His love for them He invited them to become a kingdom of priests. That invitation went beyond the formal Levitical Priesthood; it was a corporate call to relate to the Father and to act for Him. Finally, but not least, we saw that in the Father's love for Israel He declared them a holy nation unto Himself, which meant that they were unique in their relationship with Him. It meant that they belonged to Him. It meant that He belonged to them. It meant that He expected their total loyalty and obedience and that through their obedience to Him that He would bless them. Deuteronomy 32: 10 the Lord also said that He kept Israel, His beloved, his chosen people as, *the apple of His eye.*" It is a term that is synonymous with the nation of Israel and speaks volumes of the love and care that God had for this nation. So let's examine how the Lord made His love for Israel so evident in keeping them as the apple of His eye.

1. Read Psalm 17 in its entirety at least 5 times. Write in your own words what you believe David was asking of the Lord.

_____

_____

_____

_____

_____

2. What is the Hebrew translation of the word "apple" and its meaning?

_____

_____

_____

_____

_____

3. What are the two trains of thought concerning the translation, "little man of the eye?"

_____

_____

_____

_____

_____

_____

_____

_____

_____

4. Write down an honest assessment of how you believe others see you --God, your husband (if married), your children (if you have any), your extended family, your church family, your co-workers, and finally yourself.

_____

_____

_____

_____

_____

_____

_____

_____

_____

_____

_____

_____

_____

_____

5. If you could change anything about yourself, what would it be (physically, emotionally, and spiritually)?

_____

_____

_____

_____

_____

_____

_____

_____

_____

_____

_____

_____

_____

6. Using the descriptions below how would you describe yourself? What type of apple are you? Explain why you describe yourself as such. Jonathan-versatile; Red Delicious – sweet and juicy; Golden Delicious – all purpose; Red Rome – slightly tart; Granny Smith – mildly tart; and Crabapple-small, hard, extremely tart, even sour-a wild apple.

_____

_____

_____

_____

_____

_____

_____

_____

_____

7. In your own words, explain the concepts of reflection and protection as it pertains to the Father and His relationship with us.

_____

_____

_____

_____

_____

_____

_____

8. Read Psalm 139 in its entirety at least five times. Expound on this passage of Scripture in your own words.

_____

_____

_____

_____

_____

_____

_____

_____

_____

_____

_____

_____

APPLICATION

9. Purpose to go on a fast. Pray and ask the Lord how he would have you to fast and pray concerning your receiving a fresh revelation of your relationship to Him and with Him.

10. Meditate on Psalm 139: 13-18 and journal your thoughts as the Father speaks to your heart.

11. Help someone else. Pray about organizing a small study group, a support group of "God's Apple Ladies" to encourage and to build one another up, to become true sisters of faith whose hearts will be knit together in love.

The Father protects His apple gals. The Father instructs His apple ladies and the Father keep His apple gals if they want to be kept. We are His beautiful, luscious and fruitful gals.

Prayer

Father, open up my eyes and remove the scales of distortion that have caused me to see myself other than how you see me. Heal my heart of the wounds that have been festering for so long, hidden from plain view but manifesting just the same. Increase my confidence in you so that I can trust you without reservation and obey you without hesitation. Lord, thanks for making me one of your Apple Ladies. As you are healing me, help me to help others to heal. In Jesus Name, Amen.

JOURNALING

(Now write down those things that come to your mind as you reflect upon this lesson. It may help to go back over the questions and the responses.)

Embracing the Love of the Father: He Is the Core of My Being!

For in Him we live and move and have our being. As some of your own
poets have said, we are his offspring.
Acts 17:28

In the previous chapter we discovered that to be the apple of the Father's eye means that we are so precious to Him. It also conveys the concept that if we would but look into His eye we will see reflected there how He sees us, as we are to be reflectors of His own image. We also learned that in being the apple of the Father's eye means that we have his care and protection. We are indeed His daughters; His offspring. And all that we are to the Father is great, it's wonderful, it's marvelous and yet the most important thing is that **He is the core of our beings!**

How in the world do I even begin to explain this concept? How do I even begin to try and convey the idea and fact that the King of glory, the Creator of the universe, chooses to occupy an imperfect human vessel? I love the Lord with all my heart and I know that He lives on the inside of me. Yet at times I still cannot get my mind wrapped around the fact that He loved me so much that He sent heaven's best just for me so that I could be a reflector of His glory. Please bear with me as I make an attempt to help us all to understand what it means for the Father to be the very core of our beings.

We are human **beings** created in the image of a mighty God. The word **being** means that we exist. The reason for our very existence is because God is the **core** of our existence. Now, the word **core** means central or innermost part of something. It is the most important part of a thing. In the case of an apple it is the part of the apple where its seed is located. The seed is the essence of the apple. According to Webster's Dictionary, essence is defined as the intrinsic or indispensable properties that serve to characterize or identify something. Essence is also the inherent or unchanging nature of a thing making it the most vital or essential part.

An apple that has not been "cored" or had the core removed is a whole apple. We are God's Apple Ladies and that means that we are to be whole because the Father is the core of our existence. We were created in the image of God the Father, God the Son, and God the Holy Spirit. God created us as human beings who are spirit, soul and body. It was in our human spirits that the Spirit of the Lord came in and took up residence, thus bringing about regeneration that made us His own and connecting us to Him and Him to us. The Holy Spirit is the seed within us that produces and cultivates His fruit so that our lives are fruitful. In John the 15th chapter Jesus said, *"I am the vine, you are the branches. If any man abides in me and I in him, he will bear much fruit; apart from me you can do nothing"*. We are connected to the Father and being connected to Him means that we are in union with Him.

My grandfather was a longshoreman or a stevedore. For many years he worked the docks in Norfolk, Virginia unloading and loading the big ships. I remember going with him at times as he looked on the board to see if he would have work. I remember also the men talking about the union. The union was an organization of workers who joined together to protect their common interest and to try and get their work conditions improved. Our heavenly Father is a union within Himself. We have joined forces with Him and He is the one who looks out constantly for our total wellbeing. His word says that, "S*o shall they fear the name of the Lord from the west, and His glory from the rising of the sun; when the enemy comes in like a flood, the Spirit of the Lord shall lift up a standard against him. Isaiah 59:19.*

In Acts the 17th chapter, the Apostle Paul arrived in the city of Athens. At this time it was a city that was taken over by idolatry. Paul was taken to the Areopagus and there stood in the midst of those men and immediately started his discourse concerning an altar which he had seen inscribed with, "TO AN UNKNOWN GOD." Let's take a look at what he said in Acts 17: 22-31.

Then Paul stood in the midst of the Areopagus and said, "Men of Athens, I perceive that in all things you are very religious. For as I was passing through and considering the objects of your worship I even found an altar with this inscription: TO THE UNKNOWN GOD. Therefore, the One whom you worship without knowing, Him I proclaim to you: God, who made the world and everything in it, since He is Lord of heaven and earth, does not dwell in temples made with hands. Nor is He worshiped with men's hands, as though He needed anything, since He gives to all life, breath, and all things. And He has made from one blood every nation of men to dwell on all the face of the earth, and has determined their preappointed times and the boundaries of their dwellings, so that they should seek the Lord, in the hope that they might grope for Him and find Him, though He is not far from each one of us; for in Him we live and move and have our being, as also some of your own poets have said, 'For we are also His offspring.' Therefore, since we are the offspring of God, we ought not to think that the Divine Nature is like gold or silver or stone, something shaped by art and man's devising. Truly, these times of ignorance God overlooked, but now commands all men everywhere to repent, because He has appointed a day on which He will judge the world in righteousness by the Man whom He has ordained. He has given assurance of this to all by raising Him from the dead.

Wow, what an awesome God we serve. To know that it is in Him that we live and move and have our existence and that we are His offspring is just mind boggling! Now let's examine what this means.

- **In Him we live and move**… Our very purpose for living is to worship and bring glory to the Father. It is God who breathes His breath into you so that we are able to get out of the bed each morning. It is He who causes us to lay our heads down each night and sleep in peace. It is He who causes us to put one foot before the other and go where He would have us to go and do what He would have us to do. We glorify in our service to Him.

    1. Matthew 5: 16 -Let your light so shine before men, that they may see your good works and glorify your Father in heaven. Thank you Father for life

    2. John 10:10 -The *thief does not come except to steal, and to kill, and to destroy. I have come that they may have life, and that they may have it more abundantly.*

- **In Him we have our existence...** We were not created with the hands of a man but fashioned by the creator of the universe. Oh, to think that he thoughtfully and purposely created us for Himself.

  1. *Genesis 1: 26-27 -Then God said, "Let us make man in our image, in our likeness, and let them rule over the fish of the sea and the birds of the air, over the livestock, over all the earth, and over all the creatures that move along the ground." So God created man in his own image, in the image of God he created him; male and female he created them.*

  2. *Genesis 2: 7 -And the LORD God formed man of the dust of the ground, and breathed into his nostrils the breath of life; and man became a living being.*

  3. *Psalm 139: 13-14 -For you formed me in my inward parts; you covered me in my mother's womb. I will praise you for I am fearfully and wonderfully made; marvelous are Your works, and that my soul knows very well.*

- **We are His offspring...** We are descendants of the Father; we are His children.

  1. *Romans 8:17 -And if children, then heirs—heirs of God and joint heirs with Christ, if indeed we suffer with Him, that we may also be glorified together.*

  2. *1 John 3:1 -Behold what manner of love the Father has bestowed on us, that we should be called children of God!*

  3. *1 John 3: 2 -Beloved, now we are children of God; and it has not yet been revealed what we shall be, but we know that when He is revealed, we shall be like Him, for we shall see Him as He is.*

God the Father is the core of our being. It is by Him that we were created in His image. We were created to be reflectors of His glory as we are made more and more like Him, being transformed into the image of His Son day by day. He is the reason of our existence; therefore His will is at the very center of every choice that we make. Without Him life would have no meaning, and it is a joy and an honor to be one of "God's Apple Ladies!" Whether we consider ourselves a Fuji, Red Delicious, Granny Smith, Golden Delicious or Honey Crunch, God placed us here on this earth at this particular time to be mirror images of His love. Oh, how sweet it is to be counted worthy to work for His King.

Chapter Seven

God, the Core of Our Being

Central Theme
We are the "apple of the Father's eye", but He is the "core" of our being.

We have discovered that to be the apple of the Father's eye means that we are so precious to Him. It also conveys the concept that if we would but look into His eye we will see reflected there how He sees us, as we are to be reflectors of His own image. We also learned that being the apple of the Father's eye means that we have his care and protection. We are indeed His daughters, His offspring. All that we are to the Father is great, it's wonderful, it's marvelous, and yet the most important thing is that **He is the core of our being!**

1. What does it mean to be created in the image of God?

_____

_____

_____

_____

_____

_____

2. We are called human beings. Get a dictionary and look up the definition for the word "being" and write it down.

_____

_____

_____

_____

_____

_____

3. Now look up the word "core" and write down its meaning.

_____

_____

_____

_____

_____

_____

_____

4. Now look up the word "essence" and write down its meaning. Explain how God is the essence of our being.

_____

_____

_____

_____

_____

_____

5. As being one of God's Apple Ladies, the desire of the Father is that you be whole. Explain.

_____

_____

_____

_____

_____

_____

_____

_____

_____

_____

_____

_____

_____

_____

6. What does it mean to be connected to the Lord? How are we connected to Him and Him to us?

_____

_____

_____

_____

_____

_____

7. What does it mean to be the offspring of the Father? (List at least three things.)

_____

_____

_____

_____

_____

_____

_____

_____

_____

_____

_____

_____

8. Now write in your own words how God is the "core" of your being.

_____

_____

_____

_____

_____

_____

_____

_____

_____

APPLICATION

9. Write a love letter to the Father expressing your thanks to Him that He created you in His image.

_____

_____

_____

_____

_____

_____

_____

_____

_____

_____

_____

_____

_____

_____

_____

_____

_____

10. Set aside some alone time with God this week whereby you go into your room and do not allow any distractions and sit in His presence until you hear him speak. Then write down what He says to you.

11. Organize a G.A.L. Gathering whereby the theme is apples. Invite other "God's Apple Ladies" to give their testimonies using the name and characteristic of an apple as their springboard.

God is the core of our being. We were created in His image to be reflectors of His glory. He is the reason for our existence. His will is to be at the very center of every choice that we make.

Prayer

Father, I acknowledge that there is no way that I could even exist without you. You are the very core of my being. You are the reason that I get up in the morning and go to bed at night. Please help me to always put you first in every area of my life. And to love you more than life itself. Help me to prove my love to you through my obedience to you. In Jesus Name, Amen.

JOURNALING

(Now write down those things that come to your mind as you reflect upon this lesson. It may help to go back over the questions and the responses.)

_____

_____

_____

_____

_____

_____

_____

_____

_____

_____

_____

_____

_____

_____

_____

_____

_____

_____

_____

_____

_____

ABOUT THE AUTHOR

Vera LeRay Warner is the daughter of a United States Navy veteran, the granddaughter of both United States Air Force and United States Coast Guard veterans and is married to a United States Army veteran. Having such a rich military ancestry instilled in her a sense of adventure at a very early age that caused her to develop an almost insatiable desire for reading. As a youngster she would take the city bus downtown to the public library and come home with an arm load of books and would have every one of them read before they were due to be turned back in. That sense of adventure would also lead her, upon graduation from high school, to enlist in the United States Air Force and it was during her tour that lasted almost 12 years that she first began to write poems and short stories. Her creative writing led her to enroll in the Community College of the Air Force, and the University of Maryland where she earned Associate degrees at both. Vera later attended Wayland Baptist University (Hawaii Campus) and eventually earned her Bachelors in Christian Education and later went back to school and earned her Masters in Theology.

There were many twists and turns in her life but her greatest accomplishment was November 1984 when she surrendered her heart to the Lord Jesus Christ and became a Christian. It was also during 1984 that she was selected and listed in "Outstanding Young Women in America." From that time onward she went back to her writing but it was not until 2000 that her first literary work was published: CREATIVELY REAPING THE HARVEST: USING THE TEA AS AN OUTREACH MINISTRY. Vera has since authored EMBRACING THE LOVE OF THE FATHER, CULTIVATE MY HEART and THE MAKING. She was also a contributing author for SPEAK TO ME LORD INSPIRATIONAL WRITINGS BY WOMEN FOR WOMEN VOLUME 1. Her bible study books are currently being used for small group studies in the United States, the United Kingdom and Germany.

Vera currently serves as Founder and President of In His Image: Women of Excellence an international Spirit-led ministry whose mission is to encourage women to seek God as the primary source for healing and wholeness and to empower them to become so effective in "Kingdom" work that they will have an impact upon the world.

BIBLIOGRAPHY

Britton, Bill. *Eagle Saints Arise* (Springfield, MO, Bill Britton; year of publication not available)

Rector, Jim. *How Awesome Is the Love of God Towards Us* (Internet Bible Study www.biblestudy.org)

Shurden, Walter B. *The Doctrine of the Priesthood of Believers* (Nashville, TN, Convention Press, 1987)

Heartlights Search God's Word, The New Testament Greek Lexicon (http://searchgodsword.org/lex/grk/view)

Merriam Webster Dictionary (http://www.merriam-webster.com)

Study Light (http://www.studylight.org/lex/heb)

The Free Dictionary (http://thefreedictionary.com)

Printed in Great Britain
by Amazon

37830990R00058